We Don't Look Like Our Mom and Dad

BY
HARRIET LANGSAM SOBOL

PHOTOGRAPHS BY
PATRICIA AGRE

COWARD-McCANN, INC.
NEW YORK

Text copyright © 1984 by Harriet Langsam Sobol
Photographs copyright © 1984 by Patricia Agre
All rights reserved. This book, or parts thereof, may
not be reproduced in any form without permission in
writing from the publishers. Published simultaneously
in Canada. Printed in the United States of America.
Designed by Mike Suh.
Library of Congress Cataloging in Publication Data
Sobol, Harriet Langsam.
We don't look like our Mom and Dad.
Summary: A photo-essay on the life of the Levin
family, an American couple and their two Korean-born
adopted sons, ten-year-old Eric and eleven-year-old Joshua.
1. Children, Adopted—United States—Juvenile
literature. 2. Koreans—United States—Juvenile
literature. 3. Foster parents—United States—Juvenile
literature. [1. Adoption. 2. Korean Americans]
I. Agre, Patricia, ill. II. Title.
HV875.64.S626 1984   362.7′34′0973 83-24040
ISBN 0-698-30754-2
3 5 7 9 10 8 6 4

To the Levin family

The Levins are a family. Eric and Joshua Levin are brothers. Their dog is named Melby.

Eric plays the cello, and Joshua loves to play Frisbee.
Both boys are adopted, and both are Korean by birth.

The Levins adopted them when they were very young. Eric, who is ten years old, was only a few months old when he became part of the Levin family. Joshua was two and a half years old and is eleven now. Eric doesn't remember anything before he came to America, but Joshua has a few memories of his Korean foster family. Eric and Joshua are brothers through adoption. Each boy has a different biological mother, but in the Levin household they are brothers.

The boys feel special about being Korean and a little different from their friends. They think about Korea and wonder what it's like. Their parents bought them a book that has pictures of Korea in it, and the boys enjoy looking through it. They continue to keep the clothing they wore when they came to America in special boxes, and they like to take out the tiny clothes and look at them.

Eric loves it when his father tells him about the day he arrived on the airplane from Korea. Mr. Levin was so anxious to hold Eric that he went straight to the gate at the airport, found the woman who had taken care of Eric on the trip, and took him in his arms right then and there. He knew it was Eric because the adoption agency had told him that Eric would be the only infant in the group.

When the boys ask why they were adopted, their parents tell them, "We needed to raise children, and you needed parents to raise you, so we are a perfect match."

"But why did you want to adopt Korean children?" they often ask next.

"There were a lot of children in Korea who needed parents, and the agency got us together."

Most of the time the boys don't think about being Korean. They are too busy playing with their friends and going to school. Eric spends much of his time practicing his cello or working with the computer in his classroom. He has shown some of his friends "Weeds Waving in the Wind," the computer program he created.

Joshua is a chess
player and spends many winter
afternoons playing matches at the library. He also likes
to play kickball with his friend Frank. This year he
worked very hard on a school report about Pelé. After
school, Joshua and his friend Robert often play together
in Joshua's backyard.

The Levins like to do things together. On weekends they go walking in the woods. They also like to cook together. They have learned how to make some Korean dishes. One of their favorites is *bul-go-gee*, a sliced marinated steak. They serve it with rice and *kim chee*, a pickled cabbage dish that is a staple of the Korean diet. The boys enjoy shopping at the Korean market, and they help with the cutting and slicing that is involved in the preparation of the meal. The best part, of course, is when the work is over and the family sits down to dinner.

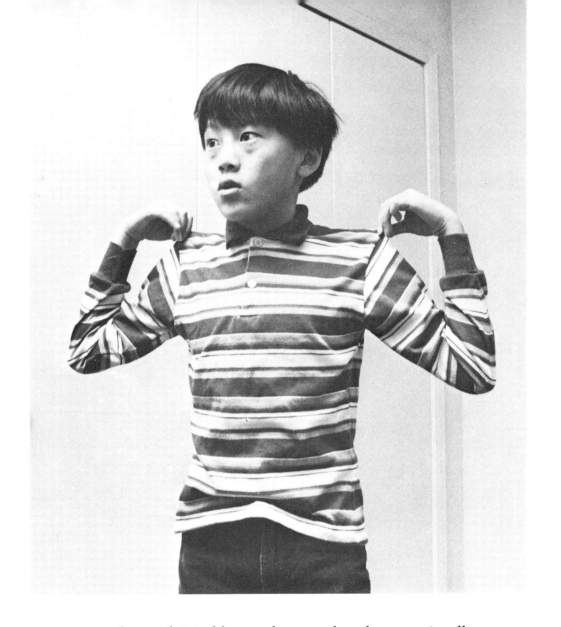

Joshua and Eric like to play together, but occasionally they fight. Eric sometimes says, "You're not my brother," when he is angry with Joshua.

Their mother says, "In this family, you're brothers."

When Eric was in nursery school, his friend asked
him, "Can you see when you smile? Your eyes go
away." The next day Eric worked very hard to try to
keep his eyes open when he smiled, but he just
couldn't.

The boys used to wonder why they look so different from their parents. They asked their father, "Why do you and Mommy have big noses and we have little noses? Who do we look like?" Their father explained that they look like their biological parents, but they didn't really understand. Now that they are older, they understand a little better.

When Eric was younger, he asked his mother where babies come from. His mother told him that babies grow inside their mothers. He asked, "Did I grow inside you?"

She answered, "No, you grew inside your biological mother, your Korean mother."

Eric became so angry he hit her and said, "You're a bad mother." As soon as he calmed down, his mother put her arms around him and told him how happy she and his father were to have adopted him and Joshua. She also told him how much they loved them and how pleased they were that they were their sons.

Lately Eric has been thinking a lot about his Korean mother. Why did she give him up for adoption? What did she look like and why didn't she keep him? If she were to come to this country, would she recognize him? Would she talk to him?

The boys have
many questions like those, and some
of the questions are hard to answer. No one knows
what the boys' biological mothers look like, and no
one knows why they had to give their babies up. Those
are questions that simply cannot be answered.

"What is probably true," the Levins tell their sons,
"is that your biological mothers cared about what
would happen to you and couldn't take proper care of
you. They must have felt sad for a long time after they
gave you up for adoption."

Eric and Joshua know that their parents love them very much. They are part of a loving family. Their grandmother is also an important member of the family. She lives far away, but both boys look forward to her visits. They spend hours playing Hearts with her, and once in a while one of the boys wins a game.

Joshua and Eric love to talk about the day they became American citizens. Their father had said to them, "You are part of our family. Now it's time you adopt our country."

It was an important day, and Joshua and Eric got dressed in their best clothes to go to the courtroom.

The courtroom was crowded with people who had come to be citizens. The judge spoke to them for a few minutes, and then everyone in the group pledged allegiance to the American flag. Joshua and Eric had been practicing the pledge with their parents for weeks.

Afterwards the judge gave them their citizenship papers, and a woman from a local organization gave them each an American flag.

Although they have become American citizens, the boys have kept Korean middle names. Joshua's is Nam Sun and Eric's is Hyun. Eric likes to tell his friend David that he can't be President of the United States because he is a naturalized citizen. "But I can be President of Korea," he says.

Sometimes when the family goes out to eat or to shop, people stare out of curiosity. The boys used to be embarrassed, but they are becoming accustomed to people's questioning looks.

There are many Asian children who have been adopted by American families, but Joshua and Eric aren't aware of it, because they are the only adopted Asian children in their school and neighborhood. There are other Asian children in school, Koreans, Chinese and Japanese, but they all have Asian parents.

The Levins are not
a typical family. No one in the
family is biologically related to any of the others.
Nevertheless they are a family because they choose to be
one. Like other families, they live together and play
together. Most important, they share work and share love.